HEADWATERS TO CHANGE

Navigating Growth, Cultivating Presence

JAMES SIMON

Copyright © 2025
JAMES SIMON

All rights are reserved. No part of this book may be reproduced, distributed, or transmitted in any form or by any means, including photocopying, recording, or other electronic or mechanical methods, without the prior written permission of the author, except in the case of brief quotations embodied in critical reviews and specific other noncommercial uses permitted by copyright law. For permission requests, write to the author at the address provided in the acknowledgments section of this book.

First Printing Edition, 2025

ISBN 978-1-7383139-1-4

Dedication

In loving memory of my brother,

Benjamin Simon

"*It was here, while waiting for my brother, that I started this story, although, of course, at the time I did not know that stories of life are often more like rivers than books.*"

Norman Maclean: A River Runs Through It

"When we look at the word 'Improvement,' the 'I' comes first, serving as a powerful reminder that true transformational change must begin from within the self."

James Simon

Contents

Forward By George Mumford 7

Chapter 1 Introduction 9

Chapter 2: Navigating Waters 21

Chapter 3: Purpose: Setting Direction 57

Chapter 4: Mindfulness– Self Mastery 75

Chapter 5: Kaizen: Continuous Improvement 105

Chapter 6: Embrace The Process 123

Chapter 7: Reflections: Merging Insights 137

Acknowledgments 145

About The Author 149

Forward By George Mumford

Headwaters To Change: Navigating Growth, Cultivating Presence is a principled-centered process that allows us to ride the waves of change proactively and effectively rather than getting hit, consumed, or overwhelmed by the wave of change.

Breaking bread with James has always been more than just a meal with a friend. It's been an invitation into deep, meaningful conversation that reveals the philosophical roots and practical power of his approach to navigating life's inevitable changes.

Through our conversations, James consistently highlights the Kaizen spirit, the art of continuous improvement, and the importance of cultivating presence. He speaks of staying grounded in the moment, fully aware of the opportunities hidden within each challenge. This mindset transforms our relationship with change, shifting us to what I call the Eye of the Hurricane, moving from a reactive state, where we feel like life happens to us, to a proactive one, where we approach change with clarity and purpose.

James's perspective isn't about resisting change or trying to outrun it. Instead, it's about aligning with it, learning to move with its currents, and using its momentum to grow. This alignment brings adaptability and resilience, empowering us to not only face uncertainty but to thrive within it, turning each experience into a stepping stone toward greater personal and professional fulfillment.

Chapter 1
Introduction

Be still like a mountain and flow like a river.

— **Lao Tzu**

Rivers have been a source of great significance for me throughout my life. There's a unique quality about rivers that have captivated humanity since ancient times, serving as a powerful symbol of life. I have always found beauty in the river's constant transformation as it flows from its tranquil headwaters, navigating through waterfalls and rapids on its journey to open waters. No matter the obstacles, the water persistently finds a way to keep in flow, embodying resilience and adaptability.

One day, on a hike with my family to the headwaters of the Bow River in Alberta, Canada, this connection became complete. I experienced firsthand the pure power and beauty as the glacial source waters flowed over Bow Falls, forming small streams that fed into Bow Lake's beautiful emerald waters, the headwater of the mighty Bow River. In a moment of awareness, nature showed me the connection to change and improvement through the natural beauty of its water systems. The continuous, unyielding flow of the river mirrored the relentless progress and transformation inherent in life itself, inspiring me to embrace the natural cycle of change and growth. The headwater of a river is the purest point, where all the chemical and elemental compounds enter the waters, and the flow begins. The headwater is like the state of mind called Shoshin or beginners mind. Zen master Shunryu Suzuki, author of 'Zen Mind, Beginners Mind' teaches that in the beginner's mind, possibilities are limitless, whereas, in the expert's mind, they are few. Shoshin can also be translated into "never forget your original intent."

As you navigate your journey, you will encounter challenges to overcome and periods of tranquillity, each contributing to the inherent beauty of the entire experience.

Genuine success for individuals, teams, or organizations always starts with a strong foundation, a "headwater" that drives lasting change and meaningful impact. This foundation comes from a clear focus, mental resilience, and an unshakable commitment to continuous improvement. With these in place, they not only achieve their goals but also create ripple effects that inspire transformation in others. These principles are what shaped the vision behind Headwaters to Change.

As I began to write, I reflected on more than two decades of hands-on experience I have gained from leading, coaching, and studying the art of improvement in my personal and professional life.

Introduction

My approach will strongly emphasize the philosophies and principles of 'kaizen,' often referred to as continuous improvement and the practice of mindfulness. The word Kaizen is formed from two Kanji figures, 改 'Kai' - 'change' and 善 'Zen' - 'good.' Kaizen embodies a deep commitment to making numerous small adjustments that, over time, yield significant strides toward one's goals and purpose. The other foundational philosophy that has supported my personal growth is mindfulness, which, as defined by Jon Kabat-Zinn, founder of 'Mindfulness-Based Stress Reduction' MBSR, is "awareness that arises through paying attention, on purpose, in the present moment, non-judgementally." It is also a way to connect deeply with yourself and others; as Zen Master Dogen said, "To know yourself is to forget yourself," which is about dedicating time to understanding ourselves with clarity and honesty and examining our thoughts and emotions so we can begin to break down the barriers that separate us from others. The teachings in these philosophies have guided my understanding of navigating growth and cultivating presence.

An artful simplicity in the science of change has always drawn me in. Yet, over the years, I've observed this simplicity become entangled in an overly complicated process cluttered with tools and ego. My research into improvement, change, and mental performance philosophies revealed their roots in the practical challenges of individuals and groups. These groundbreaking efforts by the many giants whose shoulders I stand on initiated a flow of knowledge that significantly influences our world today and establishes a foundation for curiosity, driving further advancements in our understanding.

Although we have vast knowledge literally at our fingertips through devices that have become a permanent attachment to our hands, we still struggle to embrace change and improvement. This struggle has become my passion and a lasting fascination. It compels me to consistently return to basics and understand the foundational principles behind their creation rather than merely adopting the latest fads and trends.

Through this book, I reflect on the elements that support change, rooted in the fundamental principles set forth by those who came before us.

Ripple Effect

In Joseph Campbell's The Hero with a Thousand Faces, there is a stage called meeting the mentor, where the hero encounters a mentor or guide who provides support, advice, and guidance on the journey ahead. I would not be writing this book without my mentors, who have walked with me on my journey, and their teachings and words will be woven throughout the pages.

The foundational elements of 'Headwaters to Change' were shaped through lived experiences. I embraced both successes and failures throughout my journey of leading and supporting change. As I reflect on my career, I can't help but be thankful for the many missteps I encountered along the way. Each mistake was a valuable lesson, shaping me into who I am today.

One simple and yet obvious mistake that I had read about many times but failed to see when it was in-front of me came when I first supported a team to help them make their work environment more efficient. Thinking I was being helpful, I gained their perspective and decided to do this for them on their off-shift to save time. This only frustrated them because they were not involved in the changes, which disrupted their workflow. From this, I learned the very basic yet fundamental lesson that empowering those affected by a problem to be part of its solution is crucial, even when our intentions are to help. When we truly learn from mistakes, it turns into experience and awareness to adjust and improve so that next time, the outcome will be more positive. Like when I supported a nursing team in establishing a daily problem-solving process to address unit issues. This enabled the team to identify a seemingly small problem of the jam that is often used to support patients taking medications that were not available when they needed it, which caused frustration and delays. The team took the initiative and resolved this by adjusting their stock levels and implementing a more streamlined ordering process, eliminating the issue themselves. We read about these basic concepts, but it's not until you learn them through experience that they truly sink in.

Compass of Performance

Through direct experiences, I've found a meaningful path that has allowed me to identify four essential elements to support true growth. These have consistently been instrumental in my interactions with individuals and teams, no matter the scale or context of our collaboration.

First, you must have a defined direction with supported standards and processes to support your journey, which forms your True North. Second, the focus on our inner mastery, mental health, and performance mindsets isn't just a nice talking point; it's essential to silence our inner critics and establish healthy responses to the challenges we face. The practice of mindfulness is our guide. The third area, if we genuinely want to be high performing, is the awareness that just showing up isn't enough; we need to constantly challenge the norm and systematically deal with the inevitable hurdles we will undoubtedly face, and this is the Kaizen philosophy. Lastly, we must embrace the processes within the first three points every day, even the mundane ones, which will undoubtedly need our mindfulness practice to get us through, as the commitment to the practice ultimately propels us into those rare spaces of elite performers.

I want to stress that it is important to meet you where you are on your journey, and that's why I think of these four elements as the points of a compass. You may need to follow a different point of the compass depending on where you are on your journey; just like if you were travelling to a destination, your path will differ depending on your starting point. However, the constant we can always rely on is that the North will always be true and serve as your guide back to your headwaters and foundational purpose, helping you navigate your way forward again.

Performance Compass:

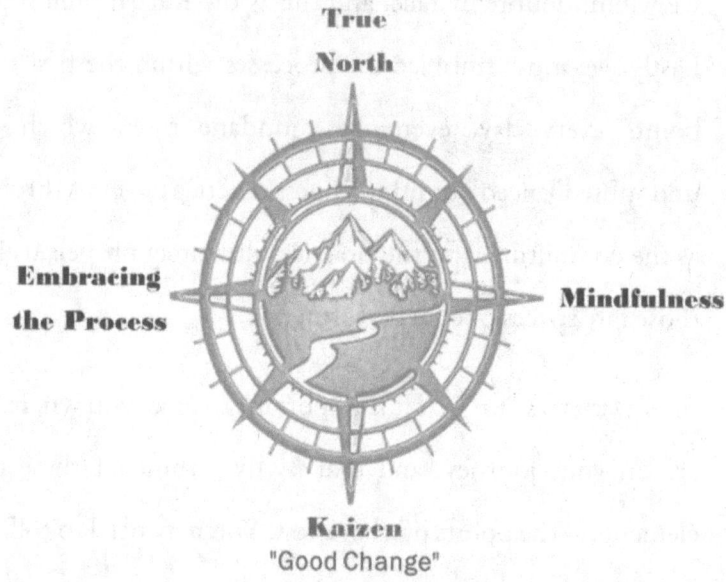

Now, before we move into the main body of the book, I offer a moment to reflect on this Buddhist teaching I first read in Dr. Joseph's Parents book, 'Zen Golf':

"Four types of cups, four kinds of students. Instruction is symbolized by water being poured.

The first cup is upside down, representing a student who is supposedly there to learn but pays no attention. No matter how much is poured, nothing gets in.

The second cup is right side up but has a hole in the bottom. We hear what's being taught, but we forget it all too soon (in one ear, out the other). We didn't chew on it, digest it, or take it to heart.

The third cup is right side up and doesn't have a hole in it, but the inside is covered with dirt. When the clear water of instruction is poured in, the dirt makes it cloudy. This symbolizes the way we can distort what we hear, interpreting and editing it to fit into our preconceived ideas or opinions. Nothing new is actually learned; anything new that doesn't match our opinion is resisted, ignored, or disregarded.

The fourth cup represents the ideal way to be a student. It is upright, receiving what is taught. It has no holes, retaining what is taught. It is clean and open to learning something new. To whatever extent you can, be like the fourth cup.

An upright, clean, open, and fully uncovered cup is the ideal way to be a student" and the ideal way to read this book.

Chapter 2:
Navigating Waters

"Don't be afraid to wander. Sometimes, getting lost is the best way to find yourself."

– Paulo Coelho, The Alchemist

I'm fascinated by origin stories, those glimpses into what shapes the identity of individuals and teams. I remember when I first realized the power of my own journey and how it shaped my identity. Embracing the power of your own story is crucial because no matter the path we've walked, we are individuals and inherently unique. Embracing this truth is paramount, yet it can be hard as we so often get in our own minds comparing ourselves to societal norms that confine us to predefined boxes that others create. It's time to challenge these constraints, celebrate the diversity and beauty of our individuality, and release the power of change that will come from it.

A relentless pursuit of growth has defined my journey, embracing each opportunity with passion and curiosity, breaking out of those traditional boxes. One crucial lesson I've learned is not to replicate others and their methods but to deeply understand the origins of the challenges they sought to overcome, leading to their breakthroughs. This understanding transforms the meaning behind the approaches and tools enriching our paths with fresh perspectives and invaluable insights. As the poet Matsuo Basho said, "Do not seek to follow in the footsteps of the wise; seek what they sought."

Embracing My Flow

Growing up in Essex, England, within a family from London's vibrant East End, I was inspired by my parents' entrepreneurial spirit, which shaped my passion for business from an early age. I learnt firsthand the importance of hard work, forging meaningful connections, and always greeting people with a smile. During my childhood, we moved frequently as my parents sought to grow and improve the opportunities for our family, which sharpened my adaptability and anchored an unwavering sense of family support, which set a foundation for feeling safe to embrace change fearlessly.

Sports have consistently been a part of my life, providing stability during various moves. They offered a platform to connect with like-minded individuals, fostering my personal growth. Whether through soccer, boxing, or hockey, I found solace in the discipline and camaraderie that these activities offered.

Boxing particularly captivated me with its graceful science of movement and intricate combinations, alongside the demanding physical regimen in which I thrived. Achieving personal success as an amateur fighter, I embraced a role as a mentor to younger boxers, something I had experienced looking up to the senior athletes when I was starting out. My coach and gym manager offered me the opportunity to coach our junior athletes, which planted the seed for who I am today. Being in this environment instilled a strong belief in the importance of paying forward the support and encouragement I had received and the rewarding experience of witnessing growth in others.

During my school years, woodworking became another passion, bridging theoretical knowledge with practical skills. Guided by teachers in the shop, I honed precision and perseverance, which gave me an incredible feeling of accomplishment and the direct experience of knowing what I was capable of.

After high school, like so many, I was uncertain of my path, but with support from my parents, I embraced diverse opportunities rather than just jumping into further academics. These experiences taught me invaluable life lessons and the understanding that there is more than one way to achieve your life's purpose if we have a foundation of trust within ourselves.

My previous experiences paved the way for me to pursue a cabinet-making apprenticeship, fully utilizing the skills I had learned in school and deepening my respect for craftsmanship, precision, teamwork, and commitment. Despite genuinely enjoying the opportunity, I was again shown that life constantly throws out challenges. Through a recession, I had the reality of having to leave the passion I loved to embrace change and take the opportunity to go back to my early experiences to support a position in sales. I embraced the many colourful experiences and always looked for ways to improve. I received a simple yet impactful lesson from my dad, who was offering some advice on my career. Within my parent's businesses, they always ensured the customer experience was a top priority and always appreciated it when they felt that from others. He shared an experience that left a lasting impact on him from when they purchased a car back in England, where the salesperson had some flowers for them upon picking up their car. This simple act made them feel appreciated and seen, and they have never forgotten it. I took that lesson and put it into action with my own customers, achieving top customer satisfaction ratings and influencing the standards within the organization.

Looking back on my journey at this point, I wholeheartedly connect with the saying, "Hard work puts you where luck can find you." This perspective fueled my success in sales and opened an incredible door during a conversation with a client. As I shared my enthusiasm and experience in woodworking, I was pleasantly surprised to learn that he owned a manufacturing company. This engaging exchange led to an exciting opportunity as I received a call from the VP of HR, who offered me the chance to lead their woodworking line. This turning point shaped my career trajectory and reinforced the foundations and mindset I was developing.

As I grew in my new leadership role, I found mentorship and guidance that propelled my growth within the organization, and my passion and drive for improvement led to my appointment as a continuous improvement manager. My journey continued to evolve and flourish and now I was able to engage in more focused education in continuous improvement, specifically, a methodology called lean, which stemmed out of Toyota.

Growth Mindset in Action

After I had led continuous improvement for nearly four years, I witnessed our organization's remarkable success in embracing the tools and the impact on culture. However, it was not until I had the opportunity, through the organization's support, to immerse myself in the University of Kentucky's True Lean program that I genuinely grasped the transformative power of the continuous improvement mindset. Learning theory in a classroom is one thing, but experiencing it firsthand from those who live it takes knowledge translation to a whole new level. I was fortunate to be mentored by some of Toyota's great leaders, particularly the late Ken Kreafle, former General Manager of Toyota Vehicle Production Engineering and Toyota Executive-in-Residence with the University of Kentucky's College of Engineering True Lean Program. This experience allowed me to apply the knowledge I gained directly to our organization's practices, leading to significant improvements.

Ken was pivotal in shaping my understanding of problem-solving and its integral role in driving success. His guidance not only deepened my knowledge but also paved the way for me to adopt the principles of Kaizen and the tools of the Toyota Production System in my personal life, fostering my own growth and development.

I will never forget Ken pulling me out of class to take me to Toyota's Georgetown, Kentucky plant. On our way out, Ken told me how many people would come looking to Toyota for a golden ticket as if you could easily replicate the results. They miss the reality that it is a constant commitment by those doing the work to eliminate problems affecting them every day, no matter how small the issue, towards the purpose of the organization, then ensuring standards are adjusted so they do not slip back, and that's the essence of the culture. Over the years of meaningful conversations guiding my journey, Ken always brought me back to this point, saying, 'Keep it simple.' It's about the people performing systematic problem-solving every day for the work they do towards the purpose and vision: go back to basics. This simplicity in problem-solving is the key to driving success and maintaining standards.

The Evolution of Excellence

To truly understand the origins of these invaluable lessons, let's delve into the remarkable journey of the Toyota Motor Company, a pioneer in fostering an improvement culture long before establishing its renowned Toyota Production System (TPS). If you're unfamiliar with Toyota culture, you might question the relevance as we are talking about performance mindsets, but the connection is profound. Toyota embodies a global outlook rooted in a clear purpose, demonstrating an approach that many organizations aspire to emulate. Learning from their experiences can enlighten us and inspire a similar dedication to growth and innovation in our practices.

The First Thread

Sakichi Toyoda founded Toyota Industries and is known as the father of the Japanese industrial revolution. His father was a humble carpenter, and his mother was a weaver. He took both of their skills and combined them with his passion for invention and built the first automated loom, which revolutionized the industry and gave birth to some key concepts for the beginnings of TPS. Jidoka (automation with a human touch), when the thread broke in the loom, it automatically stopped saving endless waste in materials and time. The concept of '5 Whys' is a simple approach that taps into the natural human curiosity that children have down to the art of asking 'why' in the exploration of understanding the root cause. When a problem occurs, instead of just fixing the immediate issue, you ask 'why' five times to get to the root cause. This approach ensures that the problem is fully understood and can be effectively addressed. Both these concepts are deep within TPS today.

Sakichi Toyoda was also a Buddhist and would meditate to help him through the struggles of invention, finding calm toward his success. You can see the evidence of this calm and focused mindset deep within the philosophies of the Toyota culture. This would come into play later in my personal approach.

Kiichiro Toyoda, son of Sakichi Toyoda, was leading the automotive division during the 1930s and established the second key pillar to TPS, 'just-in-time' (JIT) production. The focus of JIT was on having no excess inventory and having parts arrive precisely at the time they were needed. It was a machine shop manager, Taichi Ohno, who later would become the Executive Vice President of Toyota and be considered the father of the Toyota Production System, who embraced these pillars deeper and established another fundamental mindset of eliminating any activities that did not bring value to the process or waste, which are divided into three groups:

- **Muda: (Wastefulness)** Refers to anything that fails to add value to the customer, which in self-improvement could be those you are present with. In the context of productivity, it's essential to identify and eliminate such inefficiencies.

- **Muri (Overwork):** Emphasizes the importance of not overcommitting. Muri encourages us to manage our workload by taking on only what we can reasonably handle.

- **Mura (Unevenness):** Focuses on maintaining a balanced flow and avoiding significant fluctuations in workload.

In organizations or personal improvement, we strive to eliminate these wastes from our work or activities, allowing full attention to the activities that support what's important in achieving purpose and enhancing value.

Origins of Kaizen

Although more commonly associated with Japanese philosophy, Kaizen actually grew roots during World War 2. When America entered the war, it was faced with the problem that the experienced managers and workers were all drafted overseas, leaving the urgent need to train new workers to keep up with production to support war efforts. This gave birth to the formal continuous improvement approach of Training Within Industry (TWI), a structured approach to training workers using detailed job instructions and empowering improvements while keeping within existing resources.

In 1950, Dr. William Edwards Deming, an American engineer and professor widely considered the father of 'total quality management,' gave groundbreaking seminars on statistics and management theory in Japan to support post-war rebuilding. Deming's management systems are deeply engrained into TPS, particularly the systematic problem-solving model of the 'Plan Do Check Act' cycle (PDCA). This 4-step cycle of planning- defining the problem, isolating the areas of change, and setting the actions. Do- executing the plan on a small scale to test the change and gather data. Check- review and analyze the data and compare against the expected outcomes. Act- based on the results, make adjustments to improve or, if the plan was a success, standardize the results and spread. PDCA process forms the mindset and foundation of continuous improvement utilizing the scientific method, which Toyota later broke down into their Toyota Business Practice or 8-step problem-solving. It acts as a more specific internal checklist to support the mindset of all team members as they work through problems and break down opportunities for improvement.

Plan Do Check Act Cycle:

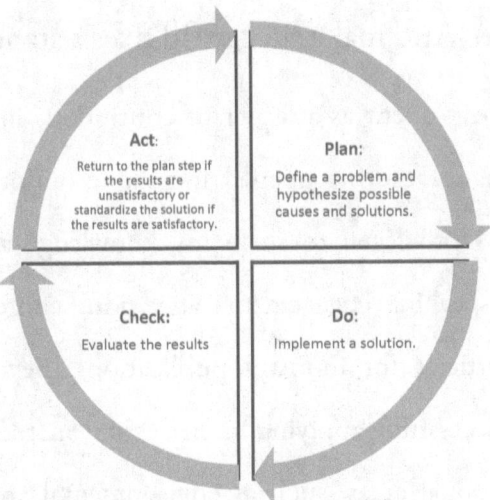

Toyota Business Practice:

- (P)Define the problem

- (P)Break it down

- (P)Set a target for change

- (P)Look at root cause

- (P)Identify potential countermeasures(fixes)

- (D)Set an action plan

- (C)Check and evaluate results
- (A)And make successful fixes a standard

My years spent as a leader of continuous improvement within manufacturing opened incredible opportunities for me. I was privileged to share my knowledge and insights through speaking engagements at various conferences and writing articles for industry publications. Beyond that, I started successfully applying improvement methodologies to non-traditional areas, such as environmental and recycling programs, demonstrating the versatility and impact of these principles. Stepping outside my comfort zone and applying the principles of continuous improvement beyond traditional settings paved the way for my next career pivot. My journey took an exciting and unexpected turn when I received a call from a recruiter who presented me with an amazing opportunity to drive change in healthcare. This was another example reinforcing True North, which pointed me toward embracing the opportunity. I now had a chance to bring my passion to support patient care and the inspiring individuals who provide it.

A Rewarding Risk

Reflecting on my journey, I take immense pride in serving in a leadership role at the University of Alberta Hospital. This privilege is something I cherish daily, ensuring that I never falter in my commitment. When I made that decision to step into this position, I faced significant external criticism, with many doubting my ability to effect change in healthcare. This was a profound lesson for me, though sadly not unfamiliar. I have never bought into the script that others want us to read in life and have chosen the path less travelled when advancing in my career against what societal norms of success and qualifications "should" look like. Still, all that does is fuel my passion for making a difference.

Navigating such waters taught me the importance of self-belief and the value of surrounding yourself with supportive people. Making bold decisions, like leaving a reputable organization to pursue your purpose, is never easy. I remember many conversations with Ken during my transition to healthcare, and his unwavering support and guidance helped develop my inner belief during those critical years. I recall leaving meetings, messaging him for advice, instantly receiving a call and hearing his insights through his unique "Kreafleisms," Ken's way of distilling lessons learned at Toyota into impactful advice. When Joseph Campbell describes meeting the mentor, it inevitably ends in the parting, and sadly, Ken passed away while writing this book. Although he will not read this, I hope to honour his memory by sharing his lessons with you and all those I am fortunate to support.

My time in healthcare has been a period of profound growth and discovery. It has reinforced my faith in the transformative power of teamwork, innovation, and unwavering dedication to excellence.

Coffee Connections

When I began my journey in healthcare, I embraced the experience with curiosity and openness, beginners mind. This practice sounds easy, yet it takes considerable effort to quiet the mind, keeping the ego from appearing. I dedicated significant time to immersing myself in healthcare culture and gaining awareness of the challenges and opportunities faced by teams and individuals. Throughout, I made a point to show deep respect for the extraordinary efforts of our healthcare providers, showing up seeking to understand and learn.

Through this immersion, I discovered an unexpected role for coffee in healthcare culture. In many organizations, including healthcare, the burden of meetings is overwhelming. Respect for people is a foundational value, and recognizing the pressures our frontline providers are under, I didn't want to add unnecessary meetings, especially as I was still a newcomer and needed to establish credibility and trust within the teams. However, I found people valued having time for a coffee break, even if it was walking to get a coffee and heading straight back to the grind. And it was these informal opportunities for conversations over coffee that became invaluable in building trust and forging meaningful relationships. These moments, often overlooked in the rush of daily tasks, are where true connections are formed and trust is built, making them an essential part of our healthcare culture.

Understanding the nuances of unwritten workplace culture is essential for fostering genuine change. Recognizing and embracing these informal moments are key to establishing authentic connections with people, especially when facing complex issues.

I loved noticing how the drinks people ordered reflected their programs. It was fascinating yet not surprising to see how the intensity of their programs matched the strength of their coffee choices. Now, I can't help but be taken back to key times in my career just simply by the type of coffee I enjoy. These simple interactions emphasized the strength of authentic human interaction and the significance of valuing everyday moments to forge bonds and mutual understanding.

We are all busy, and sometimes, we need to reframe our mindset about how we use the time we have to get the most out of every moment.

Being Present for the Moment

I reflect on a valuable lesson I touched on earlier: Always being fully present for every opportunity, as you never know where your next break will come from. One occasion stood out when I joined another consultant in their client meeting with the project lead of cardiology. The consultant had been struggling with engagement, and the team seemed stalled in moving forward. They had asked me to join her to see if I could help.

As a last effort, they suggested implementing the '5S' methodology, developed by Toyota, to decrease the inefficiency of not having what you need where you need it, allowing you to put all your attention on your tasks. The '5S' tool, which stands for Sort, Set in Order, Shine, Standardize, and Sustain, is a systematic approach to workplace organization and standardization. While this methodology can be highly effective, it's not a one-size-fits-all solution. The desire to propose quick solutions often comes from a genuine intention to help, but it can inadvertently bypass the critical step of understanding root causes. In this case, the deeper issue was disengagement among team members, which couldn't be resolved by surface-level changes alone.

Recognizing the gap and respecting my role in the meeting, I encouraged the group to take a step back and collaboratively define the problem before implementing solutions. I shared insights from my own experience, highlighting the critical value of empowering frontline staff to lead change. This approach draws on their knowledge, fosters a sense of ownership, and inspires a commitment to meaningful progress.

This meeting became a turning point. Shortly after, the consultant supporting the cardiac team moved on, and the leadership team requested my continued involvement to guide their improvement efforts. What followed was a truly transformative chapter in my career. Together, we worked to establish an authentic improvement culture, one where daily practice and frontline empowerment became the norm.

The most rewarding aspect of this journey has been witnessing the growth of those who embraced this work. Many of these individuals have progressed to senior leadership roles, where they continue to inspire and develop others. It's a testament to the lasting impact of shared learning and a culture of continuous improvement.

This experience underscored the significance of genuinely grasping the problem at hand and meeting people where they are. It highlighted the importance of not jumping to solutions or imposing unfamiliar or unwanted strategies. Instead, by fostering a sense of partnership and trust with the client, we ensured not only the effectiveness of the approach but also a shared commitment to lasting change.

Understanding DNA

While shadowing our healthcare teams I observed that when clinical teams visited patients the process being used had a very familiar feel. Their clinical diagnosis pathway was almost the same as the 8-step problem-solving process. No one was making impulse decisions but following a structured approach to understanding what kept the patients from progressing in their healing journey. I wanted to validate this theory, so I sat down with some of my clinical colleagues over a coffee. I walked them through the 8-step problem-solving process but through the lens of diagnosis and treatment, and they validated the parallel.

Seeing this, my curiosity took over as it had when first learning about Toyota, and I began research to understand the DNA of healthcare improvement. This took me back to 1854 and the work of the remarkable Florence Nightingale, a caring nurse and leader sent to support care at the Scutari hospital during the Crimean War, where the mortality rate from disease was 42.7%. Nightingale utilized improvement sciences by breaking down the problems in the actual environment, not sitting in an office or boardroom but rolling up her sleeves to observe such basic things as the patients having to eat with their hands as they had no utensils, staff not washing their hands between patients, beds were to close to each other, bed linens weren't changed amongst many other findings all contributing to passing along bacteria and disease. Still, it was through spending time with those doing the work that the actual improvements were discovered. Nightingale and her team of nurses made drastic improvements, reducing the mortality rate from the disease within six months of arriving in Russia from 42.7 to 2.2 percent, saving countless lives. Nightingale's work was so influential that her standards are still relevant today.

Taking the time to understand the DNA or history of individuals, teams, or organizations is critical to not falling into the trap of ignoring that they may already know how to support change in their own language but don't recognize it within the internal frustrations they face. When we show respect for that knowledge, it allows them to fall back on their lived experience of working through and achieving success in the past releasing the ability to move forward in the present. The focus now is solely on the present moment. Applying the teaching to the need now allows people to have direct experience again, building trust that the process works instead of wasting valuable time training people on endless iterations of theory in a classroom. This direct experience will create the very curiosity I had in my journey that allows you to explore and challenge yourself turning the lessons into habits instead of one-time unsustainable projects.

While the roots of TPS and Kaizen methodology go back to business and manufacturing, their true power lies in their universal applicability. These principles are not limited to any specific industry or individual but can be adopted by any organization or person in their pursuit of success toward a meaningful purpose, making them relevant to all of us.

The Kaizen mindset, which is focused on continuous improvement, efficiency, and a daily commitment to progress, is a powerful methodology for personal and professional development. It empowers us to view obstacles and failures not as setbacks but as opportunities for growth. This systematic approach to problem-solving fosters the development of positive habits, keeping us engaged and committed to our journey of change.

Taking the lessons of Kaizen Inward

Over the last decade, greater awareness has been placed on the importance of mental health and mindsets in performance, although it often still comes across as checking a box. Ironically, the people side of change has always been foundational in organizational change and business improvement and is evident in Dr. Demings System of Profound Knowledge, which is an appreciation for a system, knowledge of variation, theory of knowledge, and psychology.

In the fourth chapter of his book 'The New Economics,' Deming says, "The first step is the transformation of the individual. This transformation is discontinuous. It comes from an understanding of the system of profound knowledge. The individual, transformed, will perceive new meaning to his life, to events, to numbers, to interactions between people." Demings insight into the importance of the people side of improvement is often talked about but rarely truly adopted; however, we need this focus more now than ever.

The global prevalence of mental disorders serves as a stark reminder of the urgent need for mental health support. According to a 2019 statistic, 1 in every eight people, or 970 million people around the world, were living with a mental disorder, with anxiety and depressive disorders being the most common among them. These statistics have only worsened since the COVID-19 pandemic. The benefits of mindfulness and meditation, long known, are now backed up by neuroscience, which supports the overwhelming positive impacts.

I also want to highlight the importance of mindfulness in leadership, which has been elevated through such works as that of psychologist and author Dan Goleman, whose 1995 book Emotional Intelligence was named one of the 25 "Most Influential Business Management Books" by TIME. Goleman expands on the research of Peter Salavoy and John Mayer's article "Emotional Intelligence" from the journal Imagination, Cognition, and Personality in 1990. Goleman expands on five key components of self-awareness, self-regulation, motivation, empathy, and social skills, where he argues that these traits are essential for effective leadership, strong relationships, and personal growth. Goleman said, "People with well-developed emotional skills are also more likely to be content and effective in their lives, mastering the habits of mind that foster their own productivity; people who cannot marshal some control over their emotional life fight inner battles that sabotage their ability for focused work and clear thought." He also brought to light that "CEOs are hired for their intellect and business expertise and fired for a lack of emotional intelligence." Further supporting that this is an inside job.

Harvard researchers Megan Reitz and Michael Chaskalson's more recent 2016 study also supported the importance of mindfulness in leadership. Emphasizing the reality that this mindset does not happen without dedication and that the most significant barrier remains finding time to commit to mindfulness practice, a challenge we will tackle in Chapter 4.

My experience practicing Kaizen and TPS naturally drew me to the beauty of Eastern culture where the practice of cultivating presence and awareness through mindfulness and meditation has been a foundation for thousands of years. My personal journey into mindfulness began in my youth, where, as an athlete, I was first exposed to mindfulness and meditation as part of our training camp with team Alberta Boxing. However, it wasn't until later in life, when I was faced with the harsh reality of impermanence through my brother's cancer diagnosis, that I truly embraced the daily practice. This experience instilled in me an urgency to cultivate a mindset that would support my mental resilience, not just for my health, but so I could be present for my brother and others during these challenging years.

I was walking through the hospital one day when I came across a poster for a weekly Thursday guided meditation. I said 'yes' to the opportunity and started practicing a weekly guided Insight Meditation. I also started a daily morning walking meditation that I practice to this day.

I went deep into researching the origins of mindfulness and meditation practice, learning from every source I could, consuming books and podcasts, utilizing apps, and participating in traditional classes in the mindful community.

What I didn't expect was that after all the exploration into mindfulness, it would be sports that would take me to the next level. As a coach and a fan of basketball, I had picked up the book '11 Rings: the Soule of Success' by Phil Jackson, the legendary basketball coach recognized for his achievements with the Chicago Bulls and LA Lakers and his ability to cultivate winning teams through harnessing the full potential of elite athletes, like Michael Jordon and Kobe Bryant.

Phil Jackson was nicknamed 'the Zen master' through the practice of mindfulness and meditation he incorporated into both his personal life and the winning formula of the teams he coached.

As I read, I kept seeing the name George Mumford, the mindfulness and performance coach Phil Jackson brought in to work with his teams. I needed to know more about who George Mumford was, and I discovered his first book 'The Mindful Athlete: Secrets to Peak Performance' and was instantly hooked as it laid out his model of 'the 5 Superpowers':

- **Mindfulness:** The foundational superpower, mindfulness involves being fully present in the moment, with awareness and acceptance of one's thoughts, emotions, and sensations. It allows individuals to respond to situations with clarity and calmness rather than reacting impulsively.
- **Concentration**: The ability to focus on a single point or task without distraction. Concentration helps maintain mental stability and sharpness, allowing for better decision-making and performance.

- **Insight (Wisdom):** This superpower involves understanding the nature of the mind and how it works. Insight allows individuals to see things as they are, leading to greater wisdom and the ability to make informed choices.

- **Right Effort:** Also known as "wise effort," this superpower is about putting the right amount of energy into tasks and activities. It involves easily balancing effort, ensuring that one is neither underworking nor overstraining.

- **Trust (Faith):** Trust in oneself, the process, and something larger than oneself. This superpower is about confidence in one's abilities and the journey, even when the outcome is uncertain.

George's approach resonated with me instantly. His authentic ability to blend his extensive experience in both spiritual and scientific performance, and to present Buddhist and Zen teachings in a practical and accessible way was the missing piece of my puzzle. I believe what George did for mindfulness is what Bruce Lee did for martial arts; combining styles and making them practical for real-life experience.

I believe you need to learn and surround yourself with great people that lift and inspire you. That means taking vulnerable steps to reach out to those you admire and aspire to emulate and asking them if they would be open to connecting. I had embraced this early in my life, never being afraid to chat with those elite in their fields, and yes, sometimes they didn't respond back, but they often did, and most of what has really stretched my thinking and self-belief came out of those interactions. I embraced this approach when I connected with George. Before I knew it, I was immersed in his Mindful Athlete course, and shortly after, I had the privilege of meeting him in person. That experience was life-changing, and I felt like I had met my next mentor. The universe clearly felt that as shortly after, I received a message from George letting me know he would be coming to my town as he was brought in to support the Edmonton Oilers on what would be considered one of the greatest turnarounds in a season leading to a near fairytale playoff run that lifted the world with such positivity and put the conversation of mindfulness and mental health in the spotlight.

It's still surreal for me that the very same person who has mentored some of my greatest sports heroes and guided some of the greatest sports teams in history is now my teacher and a cherished friend. This journey has been a testament to the power of connection and the magic that can unfold when you lead boldly with genuine interest and enthusiasm toward your purpose.

Lessons Learned

My journey to this point has been shaped profoundly by the selfless acts of mentorship and guidance from individuals who generously support me in my life's purpose. Recognizing this, I am now deeply committed to paying it forward and assisting others on their own paths. Mahatma Gandhi's words resonate strongly with me: "The best way to find yourself is to lose yourself in the service of others." This philosophy encapsulates my true purpose and is the driving force behind my own business as a mindful performance coach where I have had the fantastic opportunity to support some truly amazing clients from athletes, teams, business professionals, and organizations in adopting high-performance mindsets and cultures that has taken me across the globe.

Now, let's start our journey...

"THE GOLD ISN'T AT THE END OF THE RAINBOW; IT'S FOUND IN THE SUCCESS AND FAILURES ALONG YOUR JOURNEY."

Chapter 3:
Purpose: Setting Direction

"The two most important days in your life are the day you are born, and the day you find out why."

~ Mark Twain

I love this quote, as it captures the beauty of understanding your individual or collective journey. It embodies the essence of our purpose, an elemental force that shapes our cultures, defines our attitudes, and propels us toward greatness. Whether applied to individuals or organizations, it's essential to understand that purpose is the foundation for a fulfilling journey. Just as a pure headwater feeds a mighty river, a strong sense of purpose fuels our actions and shapes our impact on the world.

Many examples demonstrate the power of purpose. Still, those that stick out for me come from individuals who suffered extreme hardship and yet showed us what can be achieved when you have a clear purpose, such as Vicktor Frankle and Nelson Mandela.

Vicktor Frankl a renowned psychiatrist and Holocaust survivor who suffered atrocious inhumanities was able to find meaning in suffering knowing he had the ability to choose his responses amidst the most horrific circumstances. In 'Man's Search for Meaning,' Frankl reflected on how having a purpose was the defining element of those who were able to survive the horrific events. "A man who becomes conscious of the responsibility he bears toward a human being who affectionately waits for him, or to an unfinished work, will never be able to throw away his life. *He* knows the 'why' for his existence and will be able to bear almost any "how." And Nelson Mandela, after spending 27 years in prison, emerged with a vision of a unified South Africa where all citizens could work together to overcome the divisions of the past. He continued in later years with his emphasis on fostering positive change, encouraging individuals to find their own purpose and to dedicate themselves to causes greater than themselves. "There is nothing like a fixed, steady aim with an honourable purpose. It dignifies your nature and ensures your success." - Nelson Mandela.

Reflecting on my journey, a distinct thread emerges, seamlessly intertwining all aspects of my life toward supporting others in continuous improvement. I count myself fortunate to have found purpose in dedicating my life to fostering change within individuals and teams, guiding them towards a mindset conducive to realizing their own purpose and fostering a culture that embraces challenges and failures as opportunities to grow.

I have seen endless times where frustration and negativity unfold, when we lack a clearly defined purpose, despite teams or individuals working tirelessly in terms of effort. This lack of purpose within teams becomes so apparent that without a unifying 'why,' individuals can become consumed with personal agendas, leading to a dysfunctional and toxic culture. I have often been brought in to assist teams where they believe inefficiency and problems exist because the system is broken due to external reasons, but when we take the time to define the problem, we so often end up finding they have lost sight of 'why' they are there. It has led to variability being introduced, as individuals create personal standards to get their work done, that when others don't follow, it leads to blaming others as to why they are not achieving results when truly what is needed is to come back to the purpose and define the standards that support the team success.

As Taichi Ohno famously said, "Where there is no standard, there can be no improvement." Start with ensuring you know 'why' and what standards support getting there before jumping into fixing things.

Our purpose propels us forward in both our personal and professional lives. It forms the bedrock of our motivation, energizes our daily actions, and allows us to see the true path to success.

Organizations that neglect clarity of purpose find themselves caught in the eddies of blame and ego, fighting a battle between toxic cultures that stifle growth.

Similarly, on a personal level, individuals who perform without setting a purpose often succumb to negative self-talk, leading to actions and mindsets that hinder personal development. Then, our days gradually bound with a series of uninspired tasks, leaving us feeling unfulfilled and unmotivated.

Our Headwater to change mirrors the birthplace of purpose that serves as the nexus between our inherent abilities and the greater world. Therefore, when we align this headwater with the purpose in our personal and professional lives, a harmonious flow ensues, driving us towards meaningful goals and actions.

Joseph Campbell brilliantly captures this in his interview turned documentary and book 'The Power of Myth' where he talks about following your bliss, "If you follow your bliss, you put yourself on a kind of track that has been there all the while, waiting for you, and the life that you ought to be living is the one you are living. Wherever you are — if you are following your bliss, you are enjoying that refreshment, that life within you, all the time."

Organizations with a well-defined purpose are more able to align teams with their vision, attract customers, and bring about sustainable growth. Likewise, individuals who embrace their purpose experience a profound sense of satisfaction and fulfillment.

The path to finding your purpose with visualization. Take a minute now and visualize a river. Follow it to its headwater, which represents your inner self. Can you identify your core values, passions, and talents? Can you feel joy and bliss?

Take a minute and grab a pencil and paper. Build on the visualization and write down all the moments in your life when you experienced bliss, accomplishment, or sheer joy from achieving something or reaching a goal. Begin with your childhood and continue through to the present. Try to identify common threads in these moments. These threads offer insight into what drives you and can help unlock your purpose.

Flowing with Purpose

It's so common to hear someone speaking to youth about careers or their future, stating, 'I still don't know what I want to be when I grow up.' I used to laugh at that, but it actually made me sad how often you hear it. In a global study of over 15,000 people done by Hewlett-Packard, it was found that only 28% of people said their work gives them a sense of purpose, and only 28% reported that the work they do is meaningful. This data underscores the importance of purpose and emphasizes that life is too short to live someone else's life or remain stuck in something you dislike.

This is where we can utilize another philosophy called Ikigai. Originating in Japan, Ikigai can be traced back to the Heian period, a period of classical Japanese history lasting between 794 and 1185 and embodies the essence of one's 'reason for being.'

In Japanese, 'iki' symbolizes 'life,' while 'gai' signifies value or worth. Ikigai has made a comeback in Western culture thanks to Héctor García and the publication of Francesc

Miralles' 2016 book, Ikigai: The Japanese Secret to a Long and Happy Life. Your ikigai represents your life's purpose or your ultimate joy, igniting the motivation to greet each day with enthusiasm and inspiration.

The components to uncovering your Ikigai involve:

- **Passion** (what you love)
- **Mission** (what the world needs)
- **Vocation** (what you are good at)
- **Profession** (what you can get paid for)

A Ven diagram is often used to show the overlapping elements to help guide you in identifying your purpose.

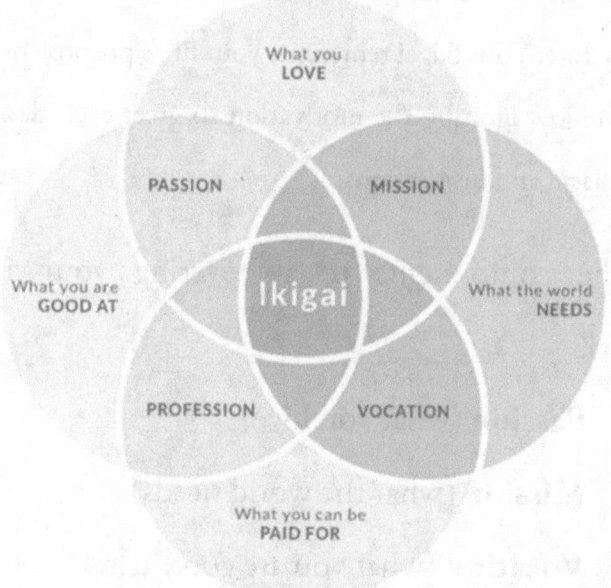

When you take the time to reflect on your journey and place your experience into these areas, it will help you understand your purpose and bliss. When doing this exercise, it's important to be aware of the negative self-talk and doubt that can creep in, and this is where the direction of mindfulness practice supports your ability to truly embrace the process.

Once you've discovered your headwaters, the next step is to connect them to a larger purpose. How can you leverage your unique strengths to contribute meaningfully to the world? This could be through your career, relationships, creative pursuits, or volunteer work. Aligning your headwaters with purpose leads to defining meaningful goals, propelling you towards aligned actions that enrich your personal and professional life.

Power of Values

Values are so much more than words on a wall or in a diary. They support your ability to make crucial decisions, coach yourself and others, and correct course along your journey. However, We need to get more comfortable bringing the words to life. Values are a key foundation of the culture you want within your team and the identity of who you are as an individual. Going back to the basics of change and improvement, I have seen that if you don't have a strong sense of your values, it causes moral conflict and leads to an unhealthy mindset, personally and collectively, as a team. Values allow you to make tough decisions and hold you accountable for something greater than yourself.

Your Vision is the Roadmap to Purpose

Having a clear understanding of purpose is essential, but it's only half the equation. A vision guides you toward your desired destination. It helps you paint a vivid picture of the future you strive to create, a future that inspires and motivates both yourself and others. For organizations, a compelling vision influences their decision-making and shapes the company's culture. Teams are more sorted where each understands their individual role in achieving the shared goals. Similarly, individuals with a clear vision are better equipped to face challenges and remain focused on their ultimate aspirations. A vision is not merely a destination but a vivid portrayal of the future we aspire to create. Organizations that craft compelling visions provide a roadmap for their teams.

Having a map is just the beginning of your journey. As Lao Tzu said, "The journey of a thousand miles starts with one step." The next step is turning dreams and visions into actions toward your defined success.

From Vision to Action

The Japanese management methodology of Hoshin Kanri, or strategic deployment, encapsulates the essence of setting a clear vision and cascading it down through the organizational hierarchy.

This method ensures that every individual understands their role in achieving the overarching goals, providing a culture of continuous improvement (Kaizen) and alignment. This is also applicable to your personal life. It's a way to ensure that you have clearly aligned activities and measures to keep you moving toward your true north.

Hoshin is a management methodology that originated in Japan. It emphasizes the alignment of organizational objectives with strategic initiatives and is based on Plan-Do-Check-Act, which was mentioned in the previous chapter.

Plan: Develop strategies and action plans

Do: Implementing the plans

Check: Assess and measure results

Act: Take appropriate action

At its core, Hoshin is about setting a vision for the future and cascading it down through the organization, ensuring everyone understands their role in achieving the overarching goals. By applying Hoshin principles, organizations can create a culture of continuous improvement and alignment, driving progress toward their vision.

In understanding how Hoshin truly works, I reflect upon the lesson taught to me many years ago by Mike Hoseus, co-author of 'Toyota Culture' and former Toyota leader. Mike spoke to Hoshin from a personal perspective of change after seeing your doctor and went something like this. Your doctor has told you that you need to lose 20 lbs. due to your high blood pressure and cholesterol.

So, we go out and buy a new fancy scale as we want to make sure we have accurate weigh in's but it's complicated, and we spend our time syncing it to our phone, setting up a plan to weigh ourselves, and dealing with the frustration of issues when it doesn't work. We might even have to take it back or get support, but the point is that instead of starting to make positive changes based on the process we would use to lose weight, we have focused on the outcome of losing 20 lbs. We have gotten caught up in jumping to a solution that has delayed and potentially set back our progress.

Hoshin planning supports the overall approach of first understanding what our vision is that we are moving toward. For this example, the vision for a healthy life could include prioritizing regular physical activity, maintaining a balanced diet rich in whole foods, and practicing mindfulness and stress management techniques to enjoy a healthy and balanced life. Then, we take a moment to understand what we could focus on that would help us achieve the vision, so instead of jumping straight into measurement using the scale, we instead make plans to look at isolating diet and physical activity, set up supporting actions to start at the gym, establish a meal prep routine, establishing a morning meditation practice and then measure how we did in winning that day. You will find the ability to deeply understand your results, not that you will hit all the targets but more that you will know why you did or didn't and adjust accordingly to reach your goal, leading to results we can see and measure. Thus engaging the Plan Do Check Act cycle. I love this example as it demonstrates that Hoshin is not just for organizational planning but can also be easily transferred into personal use, ensuring that we are aligning our activities to move us towards reaching our goals in a way that establishes the mindset of understanding the process to achieve the results instead of fixating on the outcome itself, supporting the other key point on the compass of embracing the process along your journey.

I find a lot of wisdom within music, so I will leave this chapter reflecting on the song 'I AM MINE' by Pearl Jam, specifically the lyrics *"I know I was born, and I know that I'll die; the in-between is mine.'* When I hear Eddie Vedder's words, they inspire taking control of your lives and following your own paths rather than being dictated to by external expectations or influences. I also hear awareness of impermanence, which, when embraced, puts you in the space to truly appreciate the present moments and not waste time on things that don't support your purpose.

Take time now to reflect on your personal, organizational, or team purpose. Do you really have a clear understanding of the 'why'? Do you know what makes up your headwaters?

Reflect on the experiences in your life that brought you joy and purpose. Identify your Ikigai, and begin to develop a Hoshin plan that outlines the actions needed to help you achieve your goals and live out your purpose.

Purpose: Setting Direction

Chapter 4: Mindfulness– Self Mastery

"Respond from the center of the hurricane rather than reacting from the chaos of the storm."

-George Mumford.

This chapter holds special meaning to me as it was the practice of mindfulness that allowed me to deal with the most challenging experiences in my life and discover the path to, as my teacher George says, *"unlock inner mastery."* Earlier, I emphasized that psychology and the people side of change have always been a cornerstone of improvement. It's essential to recognize that actual progress is an inside job, whether from a team or personal perspective.

Mindfulness and meditation have been practiced for thousands of years, and the benefits are well-documented and now being supported through scientific research. Recent studies, like the one from the American Psychological Association, continue to support this, showing that regular mindfulness practice can reduce symptoms of stress, anxiety, and depression by up to 30%.

Despite the positive data supporting the benefits, we still need to move past mindfulness just being a trendy buzzword, as the impact of a healthy mindset is significant. Research from Harvard psychologists Matthew A. Killingsworth and Daniel T. Gilbert demonstrated the impact of our mindsets in a remarkable study done utilizing a "track your happiness' iPhone app, where they gathered research on over 2,250 people. They found that people spend 47% of their waking hours thinking about something other than what they're doing, and this mind-wandering typically makes them unhappy.

However, some positive signs are starting to appear. The National Health Interview Survey, an annual nationally representative survey, indicates that the percentage of U.S. adults who practiced meditation more than doubled from 2002 to 2022, increasing from 7.5% to 17.3%. Additionally, it is estimated that about 6% of the global population engages in some form of meditation.

I do believe we have to address the stereotypes and barriers to meditation, like that of a hippie vibe sitting for hours cross-legged on a retreat for months, disconnected from the real world. I hear this so often when I bring up mindfulness and meditation, and although going on a retreat is a way to take your practice deeper, it is far from the reality of daily practice and, unfortunately, holds people back from exploring the benefits of simple practice. Now if we get past the imagery, we still have to address the previously mentioned and most impactful barrier of not prioritizing time to practice.

When I started my journey, it took me a while to understand how to fit daily practice into my routines. I found myself making excuses, claiming I didn't have time to sit and do nothing, practicing mindfulness for hours, or just simply forgetting and saying I would do it tomorrow. Yet, I found time to binge-watch Netflix, doom scroll through social media, or hit snooze multiple times in the mornings before getting up to gain an extra twenty minutes of sleep. My story is not unique in prioritizing external activities over mental well-being, and those quick-fix dopamine hits are tough to ignore, but it doesn't need to be that hard. We will explore some techniques to practice at the end of this chapter.

Everyday Opportunities

Each new day allows us to practice mindfulness and our responses to situations we encounter. Consider those brief moments during our commute, like when someone cuts us off in traffic. Instead of letting these instances spiral into overwhelming stories in our minds, we can choose to let the situation go. By doing so, we save energy and reduce stress, focusing instead on what truly matters.

Even the simple act of putting your phone in front of you when you are sitting at the kitchen table with your child or out to lunch with a friend sends a significant message to those you're with and impacts the quality of the interactions. MIT sociologist and author Sherry Turkle has been studying this for the past 20 years and speaks to the impacts of technology on connection and how introducing our smartphones into the physical space during a conversation does two things. It brings the conversation to topics we don't mind being interrupted, and secondly, it decreases the empathetic connection people feel toward each other. Think about how many times you do this in a day, and the next time you're out with someone, keep your phone away and see if you feel more present with the person and how it changes the quality of the interaction.

These everyday opportunities remind us to embrace a more positive and present mindset, allowing us to cultivate a happier, more fulfilling life. You don't need to go anywhere or set aside time to experience them; you just need to create a mindset that allows you to be aware of the moments every day and embrace them.

Zen In the Ring

Combat sports or martial arts are not where our minds naturally take us when we think of inner peace. But a calm, focused mind is exactly the mindset that a champion needs to be fully present, ready to embrace the moment with clinical execution. In chapter two, I mentioned that the seed of mindfulness was planted for me when I was around 15 years old at a training camp with Team Alberta Boxing. After some intense training sessions, we would wrap up by lying down, and a coach would guide us through some basic breathwork exercises and body scans.

I have to say it's the only time as a boxer I ever wanted to be lying on the floor of the ring, but the practice's impact was profound, and at that moment, I was able to embrace the experience fully. Yet, this was a classic example of what many of us experience when we are away on a focused camp or retreat, and the practice stays there. I like to call this the 'suntan effect.' When you return from a sunny vacation, you want to keep that tan for as long as possible to remind yourself you went away. The reality we need to remember is that the tan is only physical and will fade, but the experiences and memories you made on that vacation are always there for you to reflect on regardless of the external factor.

I relate the suntan effect to the camp I went on, where the experience I had left behind came back to me through the practice between rounds of a fight. You come back to your corner, and your coach has you take some deep breaths to bring you back to a calm place. There, you can receive instruction to help guide you in your next round, setting your mind to move forward to make the next play.

Thirty years later, I'm incredibly grateful to still be with my boxing club, now coaching mental performance to develop champion mindsets that benefit them in and out of the ring. One of our young athletes shared with me that while in school, he was able to take the practice we had been working on to focus his mind and remove distractions from the classroom noises around him so that he could be fully present for his test. I couldn't have been prouder of him at that moment.

Awakening Change

A compelling sense of urgency must motivate us beyond our everyday routines and into action for genuine change to occur. While this urgency may initially provoke anxiety and stress in some, renowned leadership and change expert John Kotter suggests that it serves as a necessary counter to complacency. According to Kotter, 'A higher rate of urgency does not imply constant panic, anxiety, or fear. It means a state where complacency is nearly non-existent.'

Mindfulness plays a crucial role in this mindset, as it helps us embrace every moment in our lives, even those we might wish had never happened. Within these struggles lie opportunities for profound growth. Just as a caterpillar emerges from its chrysalis or a seed breaks through concrete, we, too, can rise and transform through our challenges.

Mindfulness encourages us to be fully present and aware, enabling us to face difficulties with a calm and balanced mind. By doing so, we can uncover hidden strengths and insights that lead to genuine change. This practice teaches us that every experience, no matter how challenging, contributes to our journey of growth and transformation.

Out of Suffering

My moment of urgency emerged during my brother's battle with cancer. I came to understand that cultivating mental resilience was not just a luxury but an absolute necessity if I had any hope of navigating this difficult time. Confronted with the impermanence of life, I recognized the immediate need to develop a mindset that would not only support my well-being but also enable me to be fully present for my brother and those I cared about. This realization drove me to prioritize mental resilience, understanding that my strength would be crucial in facing the challenges ahead and in providing the support my loved ones needed.

I reflect on the moments I went on mindful walks where I would focus on a practice of the impermanence around me as I encountered the wilting flowers and fallen trees and even the rising and falling of the sounds around me, all in the scene of a beautiful morning. I mentioned that my formal practice took place on Thursdays at lunch in a session offered in the meditation room at our hospital. It was amazing that we had this available to us, but it was a little disheartening that I was usually the only one to turn up, although that offered me the opportunity to learn one-on-one from the teacher.

When the time came for my brother to move to a hospice, my senses were highly locked in the moments surrounding his last days, and I was able to be with him, non-judgmentally, just to be present with my brother. I had the honour of being with him as he drew his last breath, which was fitting as he was there when I drew my first.

In the days that followed, I found myself reflecting on his life and the impact he had on me. I was filled with a mix of emotions from anger and sadness to joy and happiness. It felt like I was running awkwardly downhill, almost wiping out to occasionally catching my stride. I'm not going to sugarcoat this; that shit was and still is hard to deal with, but that is also the reality of dealing with life and why the practice is so important.

When I was telling a friend in my Sangha (community) about this, he said to me, "That was a beautiful last gift your brother gave to you." Curious, I asked, "What?" He said, "He gave you the gift to explore and bring mindfulness and meditation into your life, and that gift will always be with you now."

In the moments that we so often take for granted, I was given the gift of knowing what a single breath truly meant. Now, whenever I bring my presence back to my breath, I am reminded of my brother and the gift he gave me to be present, to be grateful, and to cherish every moment. And for that, I will always be thankful for the gift Ben left me.

In the face of constant daily challenges, it is crucial to embrace the suffering we encounter and develop a mindset that embraces equanimity, the understanding to not value the positive or negative with any different value, as they both offer growth.

No Mud, No Lotus – Thich Nhat Hanh

By now, you know I love origin stories, and my journey into mindfulness and meditation took me back to one of the earliest teachings on this from Siddhartha Gautama the historical Buddha, who lived in the 5th century BCE, and one of his foundational teachings on the Four Noble Truths: there is suffering; it has a cause; it has an end; and there is a cause to bring about its end.

In these teachings, I felt my mind had yet again found a deeper foundation of what we are trying to attain when we are working toward achieving a higher purpose that aligned with the philosophies I had embraced from continuous improvement. We set up systems that support teams and individuals to understand when things are working or when they aren't, and what people so often describe are the symptoms of problems causing them personal suffering in their ability to achieve the purpose of the work effectively. This leads to the individual attaching to the suffering and becoming unhappy at work, which then trickles into their personal lives and impacts their overall mental health.

It's in this moment of mentally noting the suffering that the mindfulness practice is present. In practice, we sit intending to come to a place of a calming and observant presence. The purpose of meditation is often misunderstood. It's not about suppressing thoughts; instead, it involves cultivating awareness of one's thoughts, emotions, and present state, acknowledging any suffering that arises, and taking the time to understand its causes. By understanding these causes, one can find a path towards its resolution. These teachings felt so familiar to me as they aligned with the problem-solving process that had become a part of my neurological response to issues or opportunities.

Presence in Action

I remember being in the hospital's command post at the beginning of the COVID-19 pandemic and hearing all the news coming in from across the globe. We were experiencing a global state of fear that many of us had never experienced in our lifetime. I would often take moments for a micro-meditation, just bringing attention to my breathing, taking deep diaphragmatic breaths to bring me to a place where I could respond.

As we braced ourselves for the impending storm of the pandemic, I found myself in a pivotal role, supporting our head of infectious disease in preparing our COVID units and establishing safety standards. In these uncertain times, the value of being present and composed as a leader cannot be overstated. It was a time when the fear of the unknown was at its peak, and our ability to make sound decisions was crucial.

Working with teams on complex and challenging problems, you come to have a deep appreciation for the importance of showing up with compassion, empathy, and understanding. The value of being present to truly listen and have others feel heard makes all the difference in the team and individuals' success.

I look back and reflect on the lessons I learned through TPS and Lean, and you can clearly see the evidence of creating a mindful system. One story often told about Taiichi Ohno surrounded the method he used to help bring deep understanding and awareness to his students by drawing a chalk circle on the production floor, informing the individual to stand and observe. He would then walk away, coming back hours later to ask questions about their observations and learning. At first glance, this can come across as quite harsh, but it formed a culture of deep understanding before making changes, and it demonstrates his commitment to having leaders be truly present in the moment to see what is actually happening.

Inner Systems

In Daniel Kahneman's book, 'Thinking Fast and Slow,' he highlights the understanding of two systems in which we think. System 1 is fast, intuitive, and emotional. It's the system that allows us to make snap judgments and decisions based on our past experiences and biases. System 2, on the other hand, is slower, more deliberate, and logical. It's the system that we use when we need to think carefully about a problem or situation.

For most of our lives, we operate primarily out of System 1. We react to situations based on our emotions and past experiences without taking the time to consider our options or to think things through. This can be helpful in certain situations, such as when we need to make a quick decision to avoid danger. However, it can also lead to poor decision-making and unnecessary stress.

Embracing mindfulness and meditation helps us move from this system one reactive reptilian brain and allows us to move into system two thinking and into the space of responding.

Viktor Frankl famously said, "Between stimulus and response, there is a space. In that space, we have the power to choose our response. In our response lies our growth and our freedom." By training our minds to be present and aware, we can create a pause between the stimulus and our response. This pause allows us to choose how to respond rather than reacting automatically based on our emotions and past experiences. George Mumford also emphasizes this in his book 'The Mindful Athlete,' where he uses the analogy of moving to the eye of the hurricane, knowing that no matter how bad things are around you, we have the ability to move into a place of calm where we have the power of choice. Steven R. Covey has a great way of supporting the awareness of our ability to be in control of our response by breaking up the word responsibility into "response-ability."

These intentional, mindful actions, combined with the awareness of your True North, allow you to focus your attention on what the famed coach of Notre Dame, Lou Holtz, called "What's Important Now (W.I.N.) To evaluate the past, focus on the future, and tell you what you have to do in the present." This can be easily integrated into your daily routines, making mindfulness a part of your everyday life.

The lesson of W.I.N. hit home after my son William, a junior in high school at the time, had taken a youth course on mindfulness with George. At the dinner table one day, he said, "Dad, I was sitting on my bed in an infinite scroll on social media when the words 'what's important now' came to mind. I asked what he meant, and he said you know, George says it all the time. When I was scrolling, I realized that wasn't important now. I had science homework to do, and scrolling through social media wasn't important now, but getting my homework done was." I was so happy he had taken that on board. The next day, I went to work, printed out "What's Important Now," and placed it on my board in front of my desk as a reminder to me every day of that moment and that lesson he taught me.

When you cultivate this level of focus and awareness, you are starting to get into the possibility of getting into a flow or what, in athletics, we often call the zone. That space where time seems to slow down, your experience and practice come out with effortless effort and being fully present in the moment. It's reminiscent of that iconic moment in 'The Matrix' where Neo, the hero, gracefully dodges bullets as they whiz past him. In this mesmerizing sequence, Neo seemingly defies the laws of physics, entering a state where time slows down, allowing him to transcend into a heightened reality. This state was first described by Psychologist Mihály Csíkszentmihályi through his research in the 1970s. He described the mindset as "Flow is being completely involved in an activity for its own sake. The ego falls away. Time flies.

Every action, movement, and thought follows inevitably from the previous one, like playing jazz".

More recently, author and researcher Steven Kotler has done some amazing research into flow that has supported continued awareness of what it takes to get into flow and the impact it has on achieving elite performance. Kotler's findings have been instrumental in building the understanding of what to focus on when it comes to breaking down the elements to get into flow through triggers that support our ability to live life fully present, embracing the moment. Kotler and his team have extensively researched the elements that support flow readiness and broken them into these four broader areas, giving us an excellent foundation to utilize when we reflect on our moments becoming flow ready.

- **External Triggers:** Factors or techniques that deliberately induce a state of flow during a specific task or activity, such as listening to music to help you focus

- **Internal Triggers:** Psychological and cognitive factors that spontaneously lead to a state of flow during activities, like completing a challenging task

- **Creative Triggers:** Factors that can help you immerse yourself fully in the creative process

- **Group Flow Triggers:** Factors that promote a collective state of flow within a group or team setting

Even with all the groundbreaking research on flow, it still comes down to the fact that you need to be the change you want to see. If you don't put in the practice the supports yourself to be fully present with focus and concentration, you will probably experience flow without even knowing it.

Try this!

Start journaling and making notes on your day. You could even set a timer a few times in the day to pause and note what you're experiencing. Try to isolate your feelings and your awareness of presence. Get curious!

I love music, both listening and playing. I realized that studying music and mindfulness are very similar. There is endless theory and history to learn, master's to study under, and communities that share a passion together. If you don't practice, you won't grow, but if you only practice playing scales and never let go and use them in creating music, you're missing the point of the practice, just like the point of mindfulness is to take it off the cushion and into your daily life.

My ongoing commitment to mindfulness enriches my personal life and informs my role as a coach and leader. By cultivating presence, awareness, and resilience, I strive to empower others to unlock their full potential and thrive in their personal and professional endeavours. Life hits hard, and technology isn't helping that, giving us false dopamine hits and sending us into an anxious state if we don't get an instant response to a text, email or social media post. Unfortunately, that's not changing anytime soon, but that doesn't mean you can't take control of it. Being a parent of two teenagers, I see firsthand just how much the world of our youth has become so focused on screens, and my wife Carly and I try our best to model healthy habits, although we also fight the relation of our devices being such a part of our lives we can easily slip into the comfort trap of scrolling. We look for small wins like no phones at the table when we eat so we can be present with each other. Our youngest son, Edward, is an actor, and before auditions or performances, we encourage breathing exercises so he can move forward with calm focus so he can be present for his performance. The reality is that you will find you need to keep starting over and over again, but don't be discouraged, that is the practice.

Your Turn, Practice Time

Building a daily routine to take your mind to the gym can be such a rewarding gift to yourself. If possible, try incorporating it at the beginning of your day, before starting the hustle of your busy life, grabbing your phone to check for updates and scrolling through social media, or maybe before you turn on your computer to start work. For instance, you can start your day with a short mindfulness exercise, such as the awareness of breath practice, which we will practice now. The four positions utilized in mindfulness practice are sitting, lying down, standing, and walking, but do what feels comfortable for you.

Breath Work

For this practice, we will do an awareness of breath exercise. We use our breath as it's always with us and available to us whenever we feel the need to center and bring ourselves back into the space between stimulus and response. You can do this for any amount of time that works for you, and it's not a competition. Just starting, you have already won the moment. Remember, mindfulness isn't about not thinking; it's about being aware and present for what shows up. It's a simple yet powerful practice that anyone can do, and it's okay if it takes time to get used to it.

Begin by finding a comfortable position, whether cross-legged on the floor on a cushion or sitting upright in a chair with your back straight but not stiff; be relaxed. Allow yourself to acknowledge that you are here and sitting. If it feels right, gently close your eyes or lower your gaze.

Direct your attention to your breath. Notice where you feel it most distinctly, perhaps in your nostrils, your chest, or your belly, and focus your attention there. Just breathe naturally.

As thoughts or sensations arise, as they will, acknowledge them without judgment, and then let them go, like a leaf floating past you as you stand on the bank of a river, and gently guide your awareness back to your breath. Be present and accepting of whatever comes up.

As you come to the end of your practice, open your eyes if they were closed, wiggle your fingers and toes and bring your awareness back to the room.

Remember, mindfulness isn't about not thinking; it's about being aware and present for what shows up.

A Mindful Walk

As I mentioned earlier, walking meditation practice was my go-to when I first began, and I really enjoyed it. If you're able, a simple mindful walk or if you are not able to walk movement however that looks for you is a fantastic way to start your practice, and the thing about walking or motion is that you typically need to do it to get where you're going.

Next time you have to walk, bring mindful practice to it. Start by feeling the connection between the ground and your feet before you move, and know that you are standing. As you begin to walk, become aware of your foot leaving the ground and note lifting. When your foot connects back with the ground, note connecting. You can also bring awareness of breath to walking counting the number of steps you take on your in-breath and then for your out-breath. You don't need to do it for a long period of time. You can also simply walk observing things you pass, but don't bring any script to what you observe; see it or hear it and let it go.

Taking Time to Enjoy Your Coffee

If you're looking for another easy way to practice, bringing full presence into a simple routine you have is a great way to be mindful. As I mentioned, I love taking time for coffee, but when was the last time you were fully present to enjoy the moment?

The next time you have coffee or tea (I am from England, after all), slow down and bring your awareness to the sensations around that moment.

Just notice the aroma, maybe the texture of the cup, the warmth on your hand, and notice the movement in your body as you bring the cup to your mouth.

Then, be aware of the sensations that arise in that first sip.

Just be fully present in the moment.

Life offers us so many ways to practice, and in practice, we gain so much appreciation and gratitude for the wonders we experience each day.

Most importantly, we are bringing the practice into real life when you need it, as that is where true mindfulness happens.

Gratitude and Kindness

It's true that we can be our own harshest critics. While external negativity may arise from others' struggles like ego and jealousy, it's a reminder of our shared human experience and yet another example supporting this as an inside job. The antidote for this is choosing gratitude and kindness towards ourselves and each other.

The practice of gratitude is not just about appreciating what you have; it's acknowledging the positive aspects of life. It encourages a shift in perspective, allowing you to focus on abundance rather than scarcity. The analogy of glass half full or half empty often comes up here, although my improvement colleagues would challenge us to know the glass size we need first. Regardless, by regularly reflecting on the things that you are thankful for, whether it's the support of loved ones or coworkers, the beauty of nature, or even personal or team accomplishments, you cultivate a sense of happiness and resilience. This practice isn't just a short-lived exercise but a transformative habit that enhances overall well-being. It reminds us to cherish moments, both big and small, fostering a mindset of positivity and grace even during challenging times.

Let's build on our journaling habit, or as an option; you could mentally note three things you're grateful for each day. It could be as simple as I'm grateful for waking up in a comfortable bed, for making my partner a coffee in the morning, or simply for waking up. No judgment. This simple practice can bring about a significant change in your attitude and outlook. See if you can note a change in attitude from when you start through check-in points during your journaling practice. The simplicity of this practice can encourage and motivate you to incorporate gratitude into your daily routine.

Kindness and compassion practice is also a foundation for unlocking your inner mastery. If we put out negative energy through actions and thoughts towards ourselves and others, we will be holding ourselves back from reaching our full potential. Again, we must address the reality that this can be uncomfortable for some to embrace as it brings up negative stereotypes of being flaky, and particularly, men struggle with an imposed image of masculinity. It is so important to move past this and normalize talking about mental health, particularly in men, as women are more likely to talk about their feelings while men hold them in. The reality is that if we can bring about a sense of kindness and compassion within ourselves and for others, the impact will be profound.

A simple way to start is by silently repeating phrases like "May you be happy, may you be healthy, may you be safe and experience joy and ease," directed first at yourself, then outwardly to others.

Or you can integrate small acts of kindness into your daily routine. This can be as simple as smiling at a stranger, complimenting a colleague on their work, helping a friend with a task, or expressing appreciation for a loved one's support. These small acts of kindness can have a big impact on both the recipient and the giver, fostering a culture of positivity and compassion in your daily life.

When combined, gratitude and kindness amplify the benefits of mindfulness. Practicing gratitude helps cultivate a positive mindset, which in turn enhances our ability to be kind and compassionate. Being kind can deepen our appreciation for others and the world around us, fostering a sense of interconnectedness and positivity and ultimately allowing energy to be put towards positive action towards your purpose.

The Proof of the Pudding...

The profound impact of harnessing inner performance is evident in the achievements of high-performing individuals and organizations across various fields. Many athletes exemplify this through their relentless pursuit of excellence and mental stamina, continually setting new standards through disciplined training and resilience. Similarly, leading organizations not only innovate with groundbreaking products but also cultivate cultures known for efficiency, creativity, and empowering their employees. In the arts, iconic figures showcase how internal mastery translates into captivating performances and work that inspires generations.

To truly understand the impact, you must experience it firsthand. There is no better time than now to pause and take a moment to practice...

Chapter 5:
Kaizen: Continuous Improvement

"To improve is to change; to be perfect is to change often."

-Winston Churchill.

We have touched upon the historical roots of Kaizen, or 'continuous improvement,' in earlier chapters. Now, let's delve deeper into its true power in practical applications.

Kaizen is a philosophy at the core of my Headwaters. It is not merely a concept; it is a daily commitment to making incremental improvements in every aspect of our personal and professional lives.

In the journey of cultivating a high-performance mindset or organization, we inevitably encounter obstacles. We must continually challenge the status quo and avoid slipping into the comfort trap. We must be like water flowing from the headwater, adjusting to obstacles with effortless effort. Bruce Lee's famous quote exemplifies this: "Be like water making its way through cracks. Do not be assertive, but adjust to the object, and you shall find a way around or through it. If nothing within you stays rigid, outward things will disclose themselves. Empty your mind, be formless. Shapeless, like water. If you put water into a cup, it becomes the cup. You put water into a bottle, and it becomes the bottle. You put it in a teapot; it becomes the teapot. Now, water can flow, or it can crash. Be water, my friend."

It has been amazing to bring the Kaizen philosophy from its traditional origins on manufacturing floors and see firsthand how it aligns seamlessly within the healthcare environment. It has been serendipitous how I have been able to use this with the professional athletes I work with and the amateur teams I coach. Elite athletes and coaches, like Brad Stevens, former basketball coach and now President of Basketball Operations for the Boston Celtics, believe so much in the philosophy that he had 'Kaizen' painted on the beams in the weight room of the Auerbach Center as a constant reminder. After learning about Stevens' use of the philosophy, Buffalo Bills Coach Sean McDermott incorporated Kaizen within the Bills program, achieving the highest win percentage in franchise history. Even Cristiano Ronaldo posted on social media in 2020 about embracing the Kaizen philosophy during challenging times.

In moments when we identify obstacles and approach them with a focused, present, and calm mind aligned with our goals and purpose, we can trigger the flow state. I have witnessed teams come together harmoniously and tackle truly challenging problems with enthusiasm and passion, creating magical moments. Even if immediate results are not apparent, the joy experienced in the process is undeniable. Leaders, too, rediscover their passion for leadership as they immerse themselves in engaged problem-solving toward the team's goals and purpose.

Yet, amidst this beauty lies the reality that leaders feel they won't be able to stay in this space, knowing they will return to the reality of competing priorities and the monotony of dealing with reactive issues. However, it does not have to be this way. By embracing the philosophy of Kaizen, we can structure ourselves and our teams to make continuous improvement an everyday reality. Through defined systems, we can identify normal vs. abnormal conditions and, from a place of equanimity, respond to obstacles and tackle the issues within our control using systematic problem-solving. Engaging in Plan-Do-Check-Act cycles builds a positive response, forming a sustainable growth and improvement habit.

At the heart of meaningful change lies a deep understanding of the processes at work, whether within our organizations or personal lives. This understanding fosters a culture of accountability, shifting the focus from blaming individuals to analyzing systematic causes of problems. We cultivate positive habits by creating a space for non-judgmental problem-solving, where we collaboratively explore avenues for improvement.

The Neuroscience of Kaizen

There are many benefits to embracing Kaizen and fixing problems, but the most powerful is the positive habit it forms. Dopamine, the neurotransmitter that controls drive and reward, is often called the 'feel-good' neurotransmitter because it is linked to feelings of happiness and pleasure. When we engage in non-judgmental analysis, we stimulate the prefrontal cortex, the part of the brain responsible for executive functions like planning, decision-making, and problem-solving, and release dopamine. By doing things that release dopamine, we set up a positive feedback loop in which fixing problems becomes its own reward. This intellectual stimulation is what makes us more likely to continue these behaviours, strengthening the good habits we have already formed.

This process creates a beneficial feedback loop, and solving problems becomes its own reward, feeding a continuous growth cycle. The prefrontal cortex, which controls executive functions like planning, decision-making, and problem-solving, is activated, and dopamine release helps us learn, remember, and stay motivated. Over time, this leads to the formation of new neural pathways, making it easier to continue improving. These positive habits become ingrained in our minds, changing how we think, act, and feel. This allows people to reach their full potential, leading to long-term growth, innovation, and success.

Setting the Mental Stage

When embarking on a journey towards a mindset or team culture that embraces Kaizen, the biggest obstacle we face is often ourselves. Our inner critic may argue that change won't work, or imposter syndrome might convince us we don't belong. These hindrances, as highlighted in Buddhist teaching, are the root of much suffering and underscore the importance of working on our inner game to make true change. It's crucial to set the mental stage for change, preparing ourselves and our teams for the challenges and opportunities that lie ahead.

In the realm of improvement work and change management, some fantastic work has been written on preparing teams for why change is needed in an effort to create sustainability. However, this often becomes a mere checklist activity. When working through problems or opportunities, establishing alignment with the needed change as it relates to purpose and ultimate goals is essential. We must take time to understand the mindsets of ourselves and others, acknowledging the presence of hindrances.

Over the years, I have built into my practice incorporating a few minutes of focused awareness with teams or individual clients before starting sessions. This means leaving frustrations of the past behind and not scripting future outcomes, allowing us to arrive in the present moment focused on the (W.I.N) What's Important Now. This act of leaving the past behind is liberating and allows us to focus on the present moment. This might be as simple as giving someone a moment to regroup after rushing from their last commitment and giving that gift of a mindful breath. Compassion and empathy build trust, contributing to more successful outcomes. As my teacher George would say, "Arriving in the present moment means leaving the past and future scripts behind, bringing us to the space between stimulus and response."

Next, set some ground rules with the group to support maintaining a presence, such as keeping phones on silent and off the tables, and collaboratively come up with some principles to ensure accountability. These steps are important to create an environment that fosters open change in a psychologically safe space. Now, we are ready to tackle the opportunity or problem.

The Power of Problem Solving

When I first truly embraced systematic problem-solving, it was a moment of clarity for me. I had been using various tools that seemed to work wonders in transformation; however, it often felt like 'moving deckchairs on the Titanic' - it looked good at first but was not sustainable or preventing the inevitable. However, by embracing the power of problem-solving aligned with an organizational or individual purpose, we can make an amazing impact through kaizen habits and small incremental improvements.

The scientific approach of running small tests of change, discussed in Chapter One, enters here. The Plan-Do-Check-Act cycle forms the overarching mental model, supporting the habit of breaking down problems into small, controllable improvements. To further support this, we utilize the 8-step model: defining the problem, breaking it down, establishing a target for change, identifying root causes, identifying potential countermeasures, developing an action plan, checking and evaluating results, and finally making successful fixes to the standard. Committing to this scientific approach is key to making sustainable improvements.

Imagine a sports team emerging from a prolonged losing streak. Their morale is dwindling, and doubts loom over their abilities. They now face the challenge of turning their fortunes around and aiming for championship glory.

Using the 8-step model, they first define the problem by understanding their True North and pinpointing the gaps in their gameplay. They break it down into manageable parts, scrutinizing each aspect of their performance to identify controllable points. Setting a target for change becomes their rallying cry, employing a SMART goal: specific, measurable, achievable, relevant, and time-bound, to guide their journey. They then identify the root cause, uncovering underlying issues. With this knowledge, they brainstorm potential countermeasures and select an action plan, committing to their roles in the collective effort. Constantly checking and evaluating their progress ensures they stay on track. When success is achieved, they make these changes to the new standard, embedding them into their gameplay for sustained excellence. Or it doesn't work, and we go back to breaking down the problem, only this time with the valuable lessons learned, and we embrace the failure as a stepping stone toward achieving success. This team embodies the spirit of Kaizen, perpetually striving to refine and elevate their performance.

Traditional Mindsets vs. Kaizen

Traditional mindsets are often reactive, focused on putting out the latest fire or chasing the next shiny object. Although firefighting isn't inherently wrong, as a sense of urgency is needed for change, it can become frustrating if the root cause is not isolated, leading to recurring issues. Embracing the Kaizen philosophy embraces identifying real-time opportunities that align with the purpose and goals, fostering planned and organized growth and development.

The process of Kaizen helps teams navigate the complexities of any situation, making decision-making easier by providing a clear framework. This framework ensures that teams are prepared to handle both everyday and unusual situations effectively. Implementing regular processes and procedures makes things more predictable, allowing team members to focus on larger tasks and essential projects.

Being able to distinguish between normal and abnormal situations is crucial. This clarity helps teams confidently navigate complexities, knowing when to adhere to rules and when to introduce innovative ideas. By addressing abnormal situations promptly, teams prevent small problems from becoming big crises, allowing them to focus on continuous progress.

In a Kaizen-driven team, clear roles and responsibilities foster accountability. Each person takes responsibility for their work, creating a culture where individuals are encouraged to find ways to improve and make positive changes. This sense of shared responsibility not only breaks down barriers but also fosters a strong sense of connection and unity towards common goals, enhancing innovation and striving for excellence.

The Power of Understanding Deeply

At the core of Kaizen lies a profound understanding of processes. This understanding empowers teams to effect meaningful change by shifting focus from individual blame to systemic analysis, fostering a culture of accountability and collaboration. Every setback becomes an opportunity for growth in this environment, and every challenge is a stepping stone towards excellence, giving you a sense of control and confidence in your abilities.

One of Kaizen's central ideas is that to improve a process, you must deeply understand it. This involves looking beyond obvious signs to find the root causes of problems or inefficiencies. It is here where 'going to the Gemba' or the actual place where work is done comes in. This practice shows respect to those doing the work and for the processes you are trying to understand, as it involves going to the actual location where the work is being performed, observing the process, and talking to the people involved.

Focusing on systemic analysis instead of blaming individuals creates a culture of responsibility and teamwork. In this setting, issues and problems are seen as opportunities for growth rather than mistakes. Every mistake is a chance to identify and fix what is wrong, and every problem is a step towards success.

For organizations seeking sustainable growth, the Kaizen philosophy works exceptionally well. Focusing on small, steady gains avoids the resistance and burnout associated with substantial change projects. By building momentum and gaining buy-in over time, organizations create a culture of continuous growth that can sustain itself.

Embrace it!

Kaizen transcends the confines of methodology, permeating every aspect of our professional and personal lives. It's a journey of continuous growth, guided by purpose, fueled by collaboration, and sustained by unwavering commitment to improvement. As we embark on this journey, let us not just understand but truly embrace the transformative power of Kaizen. Let us be inspired and motivated to unlock the boundless potential within ourselves, our teams, and our organizations.

Chapter 6:
Embrace The Process

"The process of achieving your goal is more important than the goal itself."

-Arthur Ashe.

Going to the mountains has always been such a grounding environment for my family and I. As we hike the beautiful trails, we often find ourselves along the bank of a stream, where the waters effortlessly flow to meet the main rivers on the journey to the ocean. During your journey, you will undoubtedly encounter individuals gathering to admire the splendour of a waterfall or canyon, sculpted over time by the river's unwavering force as it carves its way toward the ocean. I believe that we are drawn to these natural wonders in the same way that we are drawn to individuals, organizations, or teams who inspire us with their unwavering commitment to achieving their goals over time.

I had the privilege of climbing The Vice President Mountain in Yoho National Park, British Columbia, Canada, alongside Sharon Woods, the first North American woman to summit Mount Everest. The opportunity came up when another climber became unavailable, which allowed me to accept the spot, and I did so with enthusiasm and gratitude. Although this climb was no Everest, I hadn't initially planned for the climb and I didn't exactly have the best gear.

On our descent, Sharon noticed I had done the climb with a simple pair of hiking shoes, which led to a wonderful conversation about perseverance and, eventually, me asking her innocently if, when you achieve a goal of the magnitude she had, it really makes a difference in your life. She shared with me that it wasn't about reaching the summit of Everest that changed her, but rather the journey she and her team had endured and persevered through in the ascent and descent that ultimately changed her. I have had the opportunity to connect with Sharon on a few occasions after this, and her grounded and humble nature has always stuck with me as a true testament to the impact of her experience.

Embracing the process sounds so simple, and in essence, it is, but it's what I see as the real difference-maker. I have had the privilege of forming connections with individuals at the pinnacle of their respective professions, and what consistently stands out is their inherent ability to perform the basics and fundamentals at a level that no one else is willing to. This is something that Ken instilled in me as he would always encourage me to go back to the basics to understand deeply and not get pulled into the fads or go chasing the new shiny things. Now, that doesn't mean stopping learning; it means understanding with a beginner's mind and then responding to adoption if it makes sense, not for the sake of keeping up with the Joneses. This is what I appreciate about the culture of Toyota and their perseverance and commitment to living their purpose every day in everything they do.

Elite athletes also have this mindset; stars like Kobe Bryant, Michael Jordan, Lionel Messi, and Tiger Woods all state a deep commitment to practicing the fundamentals to an almost obsessive level. It's that deep commitment to embracing the process that sets them apart from the rest. While we can all read the same materials and learn the same techniques, it's the daily commitment to embracing the process that sets legends apart. I think the famed basketball coach John Wooden summed it up well when he said, "I believe in the basics: attention to, and perfection of, tiny details that might be commonly overlooked. They may seem trivial, perhaps even laughable to those who don't understand, but they aren't. They are fundamental to your progress in basketball, business, and life. They are the difference between champions and near champions."

Mindfulness and Embracing the Process

The Buddhist teaching that believing in the road itself, not the destination, provides profound insights and significantly influences personal growth and happiness.

Individuals and teams can learn more about themselves and the world around them if they see change and growth as a process rather than a goal. In turn, this makes life more valuable and present. Embracing the process can't be done away from where the work needs to happen. You can read about it as you're doing here, but eventually, you must put the practice into real life for it to make a difference. Understanding that everything, including ourselves, is temporary and can change is a Buddhist teaching that resonated deeply with me when supporting personal change within teams. This is the truth and knowing it will help us let go of temporary wants and material things that are not supporting us on our journey of mastery. Meditation helps us develop Prajna (wisdom) and Smrti (mindfulness), which lets us see things as they really are and supports our ability to respond from a place of right effort.

The understanding of impermanence greatly affects how we live our lives and see the world. At its core, it refers to the idea that everything is temporary and will eventually disappear. Along with things and events, we can touch our thoughts, feelings, and even our sense of who we are.

The key lesson impermanence teaches us is that nothing in life is fixed or unchanging. It seems like everything is constantly moving, appearing, and fading. What we feel inside is just as true as what happens in the outside world. Our thoughts, feelings, views, and how we see ourselves are all dynamic and constantly changing.

This way of thinking about impermanence can be both liberating and challenging. Realizing that our identities or situations do not limit us and that we can grow and change can be liberating. It can be difficult, though, to accept that everything we know and love is subject to change and, eventually, death.

But if we can accept impermanence, we can live in a more open, accepting, and flexible way. We know that change is a normal part of life, and we shouldn't try to avoid it or be afraid of it. Instead, we might find ways to embrace change and make the most of every chance to grow.

This means becoming more aware and mindful of the moments every day. It is possible to become more aware of how our thoughts, feelings, and body experiences change over time. We can learn to be calm and stable when things are unclear and to watch these changes without getting attached or prejudiced. Impermanence also has an impact on how we treat relationships and other people we meet. Realizing that everything changes makes us respect and treasure the people and events in our lives more instead of taking them for granted. Being thankful and caring for others can help us grow, as can learning how to understand, care about, and be kind to others.

Impermanence can also help us understand and be more thoughtful about things in our lives. Seeing that everything changes helps us put things in the right perspective and focus on what's most important. Learning to let go of attachments and wants can help us find freedom and peace in the present moment, allowing us to fully commit and embrace the process.

Taking it to the floor

The word 'Gemba' in Japanese refers to the real place. It's also often referred to as where the value happens, where the process transforms from parts into what is being created. This is more traditionally a physical location, but I have come to think of it as also the place we go to in our minds.

Going to the Gemba is a way to allow people to look for the root cause of the problem, observe it directly, and gather knowledge instead of relying on guesses or rumours. This helps people fully understand the process, figure out what's really going on, and come up with solutions that will work.

The following concepts are frequently associated with Gemba practice, and I will expand this to include introspection.

Genchi Genbutsu, 'Go and see': You need to go to the place where the change or problem is happening. That could be the physical environment, or as in mindfulness, this is our practice of going inward and exploring our minds in meditation.

Observe and listen: Investigate what's going on and listen to the people involved. In mindfulness, we practice moving to a place of calm, resisting the voice of our inner critics, and avoiding attachment to sounds, feelings, etc. We can do this through practices like concentration on the breath, letting go of distractions when we notice them, and coming back to our breath, as we talked about in Chapter 4.

Gather data: Obtain factual information to comprehend the current situation. In mindfulness, this is where we take the time to understand our thoughts and feelings without attachment and then let them go.

Analyze and solve: Use the collected data to figure out the root cause and develop solutions. In mindfulness, this is our insight practice, where we reflect on our thoughts and feelings to gain understanding, which could lead to solving our issue.

Engaging in a Gemba walk allows you to engage with employees, observe their work, and gain firsthand insights into their processes, potential issues, and areas for improvement. I have incorporated this into our hospital, where managers and executives can experience what is really happening by going to Gemba and seeing how resources and information move. They interact with staff members, patients, families, and friends in a meaningful way.

When I first introduced this into the hospital, I started out in our cardiac procedure lab and introduced a Gemba walk and morning huddle at the performance board, where we made it a challenge for team members to find out what Gemba meant for a small prize. This led to some great conversation, fun and, most importantly, sustainable habits.

Establishing a daily huddle may seem basic and straightforward, but this is where the importance of embracing the process becomes evident. As a leader, if you don't commit to holding these meetings every day, even when you don't feel like it, you undermine the team's perception of their importance.

As a coach, I worked alongside the team and supported the leaders in staying committed until we started to break through and experience a true change in culture, where, eventually, other teams would come to and learn from them. But again, they weren't learning from the outcome of the process; they learned by seeing the huddle in action, not simply looking at the nice-looking Gemba board.

This parallels the Genichi Genbutsu concept from the Toyota Production System, which says you should find the problem and look at it directly instead of just using data or reports.

Genichi Genbutsu loosely translates to "go and see for yourself" or "actual place and actual thing." This basic concept emphasizes how important it is to learn about problems and see opportunities for growth through direct observation and personal experience. It encourages individuals to visit the source of the work, observe its execution, and establish connections with those responsible for it. This allows them to better understand the problem, figure out what's really going on, and come up with better solutions.

This is different from using only data, reports, or results because it emphasizes the need for direct observation and participation. People who go through the process themselves can better understand the history, the problems, and the room for growth. Genchi Genbutsu is integral to Toyota's management theory when supporting team members in solving problems. It encourages a culture of learning, teamwork, and ongoing growth by pushing leaders and team members to be involved with the job and the people who are working on it.

Direct Experience

My teacher, George, stresses the importance of direct experience through his Mindful Athlete program. George always starts his sessions with an arrival meditation to set the intention and allow the opportunity to get into the mindset to say yes to the experience.

On the individual level, few examples of embracing the process stand out more than the late Kobe Bryant's 'Mamba' mentality. As Kobe put it, "The mindset isn't about seeking a result; it's more about the process of getting to that result. It's about the journey and the approach. It's a way of life. The Mamba mentality isn't something you can just 'turn on' whenever you feel like it; it's a constant, dedicated approach to life and work."

It's no surprise that George regards Kobe as one of his greatest students, alongside Michael Jordan. Embracing the process is everything! Whether it's starting a new diet, workout routine, meditation practice, or implementing new standards in your organization, unless we have a relentless commitment to following through and supporting the process every day, we will not sustain and make a lasting change. When that critic in your mind starts speaking to you saying, "It's okay, you work hard, you can skip this time," the work you put into developing a resilient mindset will step in quieting that voice through your focused practice of letting go and maintaining focus on what's important now, concentrate on your goal, you will breakthrough and in that present moment you are winning.

Chapter 7:
Reflections: Merging Insights

"Absorb what is useful, discard what is not, add what is uniquely your own."

—**Bruce Lee**

The journey toward mastery is neither glamorous nor predetermined. It's an inside job. True North, mindfulness, Kaizen, and embracing the process have guided us like rivers carving paths through the land, shaping our growth and leading us to self-discovery and transformation.

Sharing lessons from my failures and successes has been pivotal in my journey. This isn't about superficial changes or forming habits for the sake of it. It's about aligning energy and effort with what brings us closer to purpose and joy. This approach transcends labels and boundaries, unlocking potential in every area of life, personal or professional.

"Lovely thing to learn from water. Adjust yourself in every situation and in any shape. But most importantly, find your own way to flow." Gautama Buddha.

Purpose: Finding the Source

Every river begins somewhere, often as a small, unassuming headwater high in the mountains. These origins remind us of our purpose—the source of our strength and determination. Like a river's steady flow, purpose grows into a force that changes environments and nourishes everything it touches.

Over two decades, particularly in healthcare, I've seen how purpose drives resilience. On the front lines, purpose has propelled us through challenges, fostering innovation and perseverance. Similarly, in athletics, a clear purpose fuels determination, helping individuals overcome physical and mental obstacles.

Purpose aligns our energy with what matters most. It's not a fixed destination but a living force that adapts and evolves, guiding us through life's highs and lows. When passion flows freely, we become stronger, more driven, and equipped to make a meaningful impact.

Mindfulness: Navigating the Currents

As rivers navigate landforms and obstacles, they adapt without losing their flow. Similarly, mindfulness helps us face life's challenges with clarity and resilience. It grounds us, guiding us through storms and uncertainties.

Mindfulness has profoundly impacted my life and work. It helps clients stay centered during challenges, quiet racing thoughts, and draw on inner strength. This practice fosters self-awareness, enabling thoughtful responses aligned with values.

Mindfulness teaches us to pause, reflect, and choose intentionally. It enhances emotional regulation and decision-making, leading to a purposeful, fulfilling life. Like a stream's steady current, mindfulness sustains us, supporting our potential and flow.

Kaizen: Continuous Improvement

The river's relentless flow embodies the spirit of Kaizen: incremental, continuous improvement. Small, manageable changes accumulate into profound transformations over time. Each success fuels momentum and motivation to strive for excellence.

Change is a constant in life, much like a river's shifting currents. Kaizen encourages us to embrace change with resilience and agility. By adopting this mindset, we confidently navigate life's twists and turns, steadily improving and evolving.

Embracing the Process: Relentless Flow

The river's journey to the ocean teaches us to trust the process. It flows purposefully, adapting to the land's curves without rushing. This calm, intentional approach contrasts sharply with our fast-paced, outcome-driven culture.

Over the years, especially in healthcare, I've learned that the journey is as valuable as the destination. Focusing solely on outcomes leads to fatigue and frustration. Embracing the process transforms setbacks into opportunities for growth, fostering patience, persistence, and resilience.

Like a river following its natural course, trusting the process helps us navigate uncertainty, adapt to change, and find opportunities in unexpected places. When we let go of the need to control outcomes, we discover peace, purpose, and joy in the journey itself.

Closing Reflections

The river's journey mirrors our own. Its constant flow symbolizes the transformative power of change. Purpose, mindfulness, Kaizen, and embracing the process serve as compass points, guiding us through life's complexities.

These principles are practical guides, not abstract concepts. Whether in healthcare, sports, boardrooms, or personal endeavours, they equip us with the mindset and strategies for profound, lasting change. By following the river's example, we can set our compass points with intention and trust the journey to lead us to the boundless ocean of our potential.

I hope this exploration inspires you to integrate these principles into your life. May you find courage, resilience, and wisdom as you navigate with purpose. May you always remember the river's journey as a source of guidance and inspiration.

"No man ever steps in the same river twice, for it's not the same river, and he's not the same man."

Heraclitus

Acknowledgments

This book would not exist without the collective contributions of those who have walked alongside me. To all who have touched my life, whether mentioned here or not, I thank you. Your presence has shaped my path, and I am forever grateful.

My family:

The love of my life, Carly. Thank you for never giving up on me or our dreams. Your unwavering support and patience with my endless hours pursuing my dreams gave me the green light to shoot for the stars, and I am blessed we are on this journey together.

My sons, William and Edward, you inspire me every day, keeping me humble and on my toes. Never stop being unapologetically yourselves, pursuing your passions, and defining success on your terms.

My Mum, Denise, and Dad, Dennis, thank you for teaching me to embrace change and take risks. In the face of heartache and loss, you showed love and resilience and reminded me, through action, that we must never give up and that there's always time for another cup of tea.

Ben, my brother, this one is hard. I wish more than anything that I didn't have to dedicate this to your memory. You live on in the lessons you taught me and the moments we shared.

To my extended family, near and far, there are too many to name, but your love and support mean everything to me.

To my friends, who have stood by me through every adventure, no matter how crazy, thank you for showing up, always without judgment.

My mentors and coaches:

George Mumford, my dear friend, I am blessed to have your guidance, teaching, and love. I am so grateful for the time you took to review my book, and I am honoured by your forward.

Ken Kreafle, your guidance and friendship came to me at a key time in my life. Your calm voice is always there when I need it. Rest in Peace, my friend.

To my coaches, who supported me as a young athlete and believed in my potential. A special acknowledgment to South Side Legion Boxing Club and the late John Andersen, who saw in me my coaching potential and gave me my first coaching opportunity at 17. I still carry the small pewter boxing glove you gave me, and it is my reminder to always keep fighting.

Organizations and Clients I've Had the Privilege to Work With

There are so many individuals who shaped my life that it would be tough to name you all. I am so grateful for all the opportunities and lessons I have learned throughout my career, and I thank you all.

Gord Wiebe you saw something in a young salesman and, in doing so, changed the course of my journey. Thank you.

I want to give special thanks to my healthcare family, the University of Alberta Hospital, and all those on our broader team across the province. I am humbled to serve you.

To my clients whom I have the opportunity to support, it's an honour to be a part of your story.

With Gratitude,

J Simon

About The Author

James Simon's passion for coaching, mindfulness, and growth began in athletics, where he discovered the power of discipline, resilience, and teamwork. After transitioning into business and healthcare, James honed his unique ability to blend Kaizen with mindfulness, helping individuals and teams unlock their potential. His journey into continuous improvement began in 2004 while working in manufacturing, where he embraced the principles of efficiency, growth, and transformation and was recruited into healthcare in 2010. In 2015, his focus shifted to mindfulness and meditation, and he has since deepened his practice through retreats and visiting monasteries in Japan.

A pivotal moment in his journey came in 2020 when he founded Headwaters to Change, a platform dedicated to supporting people on their path to self-mastery through the integration of Kaizen philosophy and mindfulness practices.

James's work has spanned continents and industries. At the University of Alberta Hospital, he leads transformative change that fosters innovation and growth. He has also been privileged to contribute to non-profit efforts in Rwanda and Kenya, broadening his perspective on global impact. A key influence in his journey has been George Mumford, a renowned performance coach whose work with NBA legends like Michael Jordan and Kobe Bryant brought mindfulness into the heart of high-performance sports. Drawing from his teachings, James integrates mindfulness and inner mastery

About The Author

into his coaching approach, empowering individuals to break through limitations and reach new heights.

James also draws from mentorship with Toyota leaders, where he refined his ability to apply continuous improvement principles to all aspects of life. He combines these teachings with the insights he's gained from studying with Mumford and other thought leaders to create a unique and powerful coaching experience.

Whether working with senior executives, athletes, or healthcare teams, James is known for creating a space where transformation feels possible—and often inevitable. His ability to guide others toward clarity, focus, and meaningful change has earned him a reputation as a trusted partner in helping people achieve extraordinary results.

James lives in Edmonton, Alberta, Canada, where he is relentlessly driven by his purpose: guiding individuals and teams to surpass their own expectations and achieve transformative growth.

www.headwaterstochange.com

About The Author

www.ingramcontent.com/pod-product-compliance
Lightning Source LLC
LaVergne TN
LVHW031615060526
838200LV00007B/218